INHERITING PARADISE

INHERITING PARADISE

Meditations on Gardening

VIGEN GUROIAN

Inheriting Paradise

Meditations on Gardening

Vigen Guroian

William B. Eerdmans Publishing Company
Grand Rapids, Michigan / Cambridge, U.K.

© 1999 Wm. B. Eerdmans Publishing Co.
255 Jefferson Ave. S.E., Grand Rapids, Michigan 49503 /
P.O. Box 163, Cambridge CB3 9PU U.K.
All rights reserved

Printed in the United States of America

03 02 01 00 99   7 6 5 4 3 2

Library of Congress Cataloging-in-Publication Data

Guroian, Vigen.
Inheriting paradise: meditations on gardening / Vigen Guroian.
p.   cm.
ISBN 0-8028-4588-6 (pbk.: alk. paper)
1. Gardeners — Religious life — Meditations.
2. Gardens — Religious aspects — Christianity — Meditations.
3. Christian life — Orthodox Eastern authors.
I. Title.
BV4596.G36G87   1999
242 — dc21   99-18023
CIP

The author and publisher gratefully acknowledge permission to reprint
copyrighted works listed in the Acknowledgments section (p. 93), which
constitutes an extension of the copyright page.

Scripture quotations marked "NKJV" are taken from the New King James
Version. Copyright © 1979, 1980, 1982 by Thomas Nelson, Inc. Used by
permission. All rights reserved.

Scripture quotations marked "NRSV" are from the New Revised Version of
the Bible, copyrighted 1989 by the Division of Christian Education of the
National Council of the Churches of Christ in the United States of America, and are used by permission. All rights reserved.

Scripture quotations marked "NEB" are from the New English Bible, copyright © The Delegates of the Oxford University Press and The Syndics of
the Cambridge University Press, 1961, 1970. All rights reserved.

Scripture quotations market "REB" are from the Revised English Bible with
the Apocrypha, copyright © Oxford University Press and Cambridge University Press 1989.

"Their life shall become like a watered garden."

Jeremiah 31:12, NRSV

To June

who makes our home a watered garden

Contents

Preface

GARDENS FILL my earliest childhood memories. So I suppose it shouldn't be surprising that in my middle years I felt moved to write these meditations on gardening. My father, Armen Guroian, grew up in Bridgewater, Massachusetts, and his father, Stepan, worked in a shoe factory that employed immigrants of Portuguese, Italian, Polish, Lithuanian, and Armenian descent. Until I was five years of age, my parents, my younger brother Michael, and I lived in an apartment building in New Rochelle, New York. When I was five years old we moved to Stamford, Connecticut. But I can recall vividly the long, ever so long, car trips from New Rochelle to Bridgewater in the early years.

My grandparents rented the second floor of a

two-story, wood-frame house that had lots of land around it, on which my grandfather grew a vegetable garden next to someone else's chicken coops. In the midst of that garden stood an old wooden shed. It contained a workshop, a cot, and my grandfather's gardening tools. The musty smell of that shed lingers in my memory every bit as strongly and evocatively as the scents of my mother's perfume, the roses and lilac trees that grew beside our house in Stamford, and the burning incense at church.

During our years in New Rochelle, my father did not have a garden of his own. But I had a spot in the small backyard of the house next door in which my friend, Stevie Fishkin, lived. My "garden" was beside a tall tree that in summer gave welcome shade. Into that spot I transplanted vines and wildflowers that others would call weeds. I also kept, or thought I kept — for they were quite free — a small menagerie of ladybugs, caterpillars, and earthworms.

Our home in Stamford had a half acre of land; and as soon as we moved in my father dug up vegetable and flower beds everywhere. There was an especially large bed in a sunny, well-drained spot in which my father planted tomatoes, peppers, eggplants, and corn. We used to let my guinea pig loose in it in the morning, and whistle at evening to call him home. My father had a smaller plot for cucum-

bers and squash in a low and partially shaded corner
of the yard. I remember one year when a hurricane
filled the garden up with three feet of water, so that
I went swimming with the cucumbers and the
squashes. My mother kept annual and perennial
flower borders along the length of our front porch
and beside a hedge that divided our yard from the
Wilsons' yard. My father transplanted roots from
my grandfather's rhubarb to a bed in our backyard.
And every spring I would dip the ruby red stems of
that rhubarb into a bowl of sugar and savor its refreshing sweet and sour juice. Descendants of that
rhubarb grow in my garden in Reisterstown, Maryland; and they will travel with us to whatever new
home my wife June and I may move in future years.

Neither my grandfather's nor my father's garden
compared, however, with the raised-bed, irrigated
garden paradise of a man named Manoog, whom we
always visited on our trips to Bridgewater. Manoog
is Armenian for "little male child." But I remember
Manoog as a small, wiry old man with big, callused
hands, dressed in denim overalls and a plaid shirt,
who moved around his garden with the speed and
agility of a sprite. The vegetables and flowers in
Baron Manoog's garden — for that is what we called
him, Baron Manoog — grew twice as big and beautiful as those in my grandfather's and my father's gar-

dens. Baron Manoog swore by the manure of his prized Rhode Island hens. He was an early practitioner of organic gardening.

Even to this day, the ultimate compliments my father gives my garden are when he pronounces: "This would have made Baron Manoog proud!" Or "Just like Baron Manoog!" Baron Manoog's garden is an emblem of my childhood, a place of abundance and color and design with overwhelming scents and aromas, sweet and pungent, that awakened all of my senses.

My own garden has become the measure of my years that gives me the strongest and most concrete sense of connection with life and passage through it. Yet only as I wrote about this experience did I begin to realize just how important gardens have been in my life and in the lives of so many other people, even colleagues in the academy, who otherwise might be imagined to spend all of their wakeful moments among books.

About five years ago, I was asked to prepare a presentation for a conference on ecology and Eastern Orthodox Christianity. During the weeks preceding the conference, I was busy in my garden pulling up tomato stakes, cutting back the asparagus, and covering some of the less hardy perennials with a winter mulch. In the midst of putting my garden to bed for the winter, I started to think about what I might say at the conference. And so the theme of the garden emerged, and I wrote the first of these meditations. Subsequently, I showed this piece to David Heim at *The Christian Century* magazine and proposed to him a series of essays on the theme of the "Christian Gardener," written along the lines of the liturgical year. Four of the seven meditations were published in *The Christian Century* during 1996, some under different titles and all reworked since that time. These include the meditations entitled "Inheriting Paradise," "Lenten Spring," "Fruits of Pentecost," and "Mary in the Garden." I want to thank David Heim and *The Christian Century* for their initial interest in these compositions and for granting permission to include them in this book.

During the past several years, many persons have told me how much they enjoyed reading *The Christian Century* pieces and that they shared them with family and friends. The garden is a personal place of retreat and delight and labor for many people. Gardening helps them collect themselves, much like the activity of praying. For rich and poor — it does not make a difference — a garden is a place where body and soul are in harmony.

These meditations are quite personal. Yet I did not find it uncomfortable to expose my own inner life through them. It was like taking a friend or visitor on a stroll through the "real things." My publisher has given me the opportunity to share these compositions with many other persons who live with gardens in their lives. Thus, I especially want to thank Jon Pott, Editor-in-Chief at Eerdmans, who took a special interest in this writing right from the start, and Anne Salsich, also at Eerdmans and a gardener herself, who made certain that *Inheriting Paradise* would be a beautiful book.

I suppose that the writing in this book falls into the category of what we nowadays call Christian spirituality. Nevertheless, I do not think that these meditations are vague or esoteric. Rather, they embrace the concrete and the ordinary, while also being seriously theological. In them I state what I really think about God and my relation to his creation. Yet the exercise of writing these meditations was also a process of discovery of God, self, and world. More than in any of my professional writing, I was surprised by my own words and what I gave to expression.

Through these meditations I have endeavored to capture the earthiness and sacramental character of the Christian faith. I have tried to bring together the experience of space and time through the cycle of the seasons in the garden and relate this fundamental human experience to the cycle of the church year. But it was the garden that gave me insight into the cycle of the church year and deepened my experience of the great feasts of the church, and not the other way around.

Through this writing I have also transformed forever my own experience of the garden. I suppose I have awakened to the whole of what gardening means to me. For this reason, the garden now gives me more delight and pleasure than ever before. I sincerely hope that something similar may be the reward for you my reader.

Reisterstown, Maryland   VIGEN GUROIAN
Lent 1999

Inheriting Paradise

one

A garden is a lovesome thing, God wot!
Rose plot,
Fringed pool,
Ferned grot —
The veriest school
Of peace; and yet the fool
Contends that God is not —
Not God! in garden! when eve is cool?
Nay, But I have a sign;
'Tis very sure God walks in mine.

Thomas Edward Brown, "My Garden"

I AM A THEOLOGIAN and a college professor. I like being both. But what I really love to do — what I get exquisite pleasure from doing — is to garden. I think that gardening is nearer to godliness than theology. I certainly desire the presence of God. But I want the tomatoes and squash, also the wild geese and the chickadees who in winter enjoy a repast of the seeds that have fallen on the ground. The geese and the chickadees don't know this, but I think of them as a part of my garden. I think if we all gardened more, they and all of the other birds that fly in the air above and light in my garden below would be better off. I know that God values them no less than I do. So when I plant in spring I also hope to taste of God in fruit of summer sun and sight of feathered friends.

Even in desolate January when I look over the

3

gray and frozen earth, I dream of green paradise. The prophet Ezekiel says: "The land now desolate will be tilled, instead of lying waste for every passer-by to see. Everyone will say that this land which was waste has become like a garden of Eden" (Ezekiel 36:34-35, REB). That is my hope when I garden.

But don't get me wrong. I am not a romantic about such things. I take long hikes with Scarlett, my Irish setter, through a beautiful lay of woods and meadows near our home, where rare and unusual wildflowers grow on sparse rocky soil. Romantics say they find God in nature, and maybe they do. But one might just as easily not find God in nature, only nature itself. Our natural surroundings, however, possess the remarkable capacity to rouse us from an insensate slothfulness that sin has brought about. When I go hiking, the sylvan beauty alone is not what stimulates my senses. There is the ache in the legs and the deep breathing of the hillside climb, the discomforting dampness of morning dew on my clothes, and the soiled sweat of afternoon sun on my brow.

When I garden it is nearly the same. In March I labor with spade and hoe and plant peas and cabbage in the cold damp clumps of earth. By June the peas and cabbage are ready, but the weeds have sprung up too and the insects have arrived. I can hardly keep up with these invaders of my impossible paradise. In the heat of summer sun the sweat streams down my back. I am the first Adam expelled from Eden, not the second Adam in paradise.

The Christian knows that while tending the garden there are no easy strolls with God. It is not that gardening is valueless or purposeless or wants of reward. But the fruit of sweet communion comes after the gall and the vinegar. The mystical enjoyment comes not without the toilsome struggle of raking and sowing and pulling up the weeds. In my garden the thistle grows more easily than the primrose. Sin grows in my body more readily than purity, and the keys to my garden do not admit me back through Eden's gate. Nevertheless, my garden is a place away from that first home, a spot where labor lends substance to my living while I am in this mortal frame. Birth and renewal are signs that anticipate and foreshadow paradise.

The seventeenth-century writer William Coles comments: "As for recreating if man be wearied with over-much study (for study is a weariness to the Flesh as Solomon by experience can tell you) there is no better place in the world to recreate himself than in a garden, there be no sence but may be delighted therein." An academic can relate to that weariness of study, a gardener to Coles's delight in the experience of the senses in the garden.

Many voices in our day accuse the Christian faith of erecting a barrier between "superior" human beings and "inferior" nature, and fostering a science that views nature as something to be used and overcome in order to build the city of God, or at least the Elysian tracts of suburbia. In *Why We Garden,* Jim Nollman contends that "neither Judaism nor Christianity teaches us that nature is alive and capable of interceding in our lives in a positive, spiritually enhancing manner. We have never been taught what it means for us to commune with trees, to treat other species as peers with rights, to relate to mountains as animate, to live in balance with the air, to feel the pulse of the ocean in our own blood. We never have experienced a sense of give-and-take with the soil and the rocks."

I do not know how literal Nollman is wanting to be. I suspect, however, that his real knowledge of biblical faith is limited. Otherwise, how could he forget the psalmist's intimacy with both God and nature?

Praise the Lord from the heavens;
    praise him in the heights above.
Praise him, all his angels;

6

praise him, all his hosts.
Praise him, sun and moon;
    praise him, all you shining stars!
. . . .

Praise the Lord from the earth,
    you sea monsters and ocean depths;
fire and hail, snow and ice,
    gales of wind that obey his voice.
all mountains and hills;
    all fruit trees and cedars;
wild animals and all cattle;
    creeping creatures and winged birds.

Psalm 148:1-3, 7-10, REB

When I garden, earth and earthworm pass between my fingers and I realize that I am made of the
same stuff. When I pinch the cucumber vine and the
water drips from capillaries to soil, I can feel the blood
coursing through my body. Man is a microcosm in
whose flesh resonates and reverberates the pulse of
the whole creation, in whose mind creation comes to
consciousness, and through whose imagination and
will God wants to heal and reconcile everthing that
sin has wounded and put in disharmony.

Earth, sweet Earth, sweet landscape,
    with leavès throng

And louchèd low grass, heaven that dost appeal
To, with no tongue to plead, no heart to feel;
That canst but only be, but dost that long —
   . . . .

And what is Earth's eye, tongue,
       or heart else, where
Else, but in dear and dogged man? —
       Ah, the heir
To his own selfbent so bound, so tied
       to his turn,

To thriftless reave both our rich round
       world bare
And none reck of world after, this bids wear
Earth brows of such care, care and dear concern.
       Gerard Manley Hopkins, "Ribblesdale"

My son Rafi is enchanted with cyberspace. But
we are not disembodied mind or spirit, we are our
bodies — cruising the Internet won't teach us that.
It may even trick us into thinking that having a body
and a place is not important. Gardening teaches us
differently. I do not mean industrial mechanized
farming, I mean the kind of gardening that any one
of us can do with his hands and feet and the simplest
tools.

I am an Armenian Orthodox believer and theologian. The Orthodox faith is a sacramental faith, and I have been trying to express its sacramental vision. When Orthodox Christians perform the great rite of the blessing of the water by ocean beach or riverbank, they behave, as the Armenian liturgy says, like the holy apostles who became "cleansers of the whole world." While God might have driven Adam and Eve out of the Garden of Paradise, God still ensured that the living waters issuing from the garden continued to irrigate the whole earth and cleanse its polluted streams and lakes. When we bless water, we acknowledge God's grace and desire to cleanse the world and make it paradise.

Water is the blood of creation. Our own bodies are eighty percent water. Water is also the element of baptism. St. Thomas Aquinas said: "Because water is transparent, it can receive light; and so it is fitting that it should be used in baptism, inasmuch as it is the sacrament of faith." By cleansing the water we make it clear again. By expelling the demonic pollutants we ready it for greater service to God. We tend not only the garden that we call nature but also the

9

garden that is ourselves, insofar as we are constituted of water and are born anew by it.

We ought not to draw a line that neatly marks off nature from humankind. This is a modern heresy that we have inherited from the Enlightenment. Contrary to environmentalists' accusations of anthropocentrism, Christians believe that human beings are especially responsible for tending the creation. This is because God has endowed human beings alone among God's creatures with the rational and imaginative capacities to envision the good of everything and to see that that good is respected. This is no less a responsibility than the duty to care for our own bodies as temples of the Holy Spirit. God has given human beings this responsibility as an emblem of his own great love for all of creation. The fourth-century church father St. Ephrem the Syrian says in his *Hymns on Paradise:*

> The fool, who is unwilling to realize
>> his honorable state,
> prefers to become just an animal,
>> rather than a man,
> so that, without incurring judgment,
>> he may serve naught but his lusts.
> But had there been sown in animals
>> just a little

of the sense of discernment,
    then long ago would the wild asses
      have lamented
and wept at their not
    having been human.

St. Ephrem does not condone an ecologically destructive anthropocentrism. He does not say that human beings are masters over creation with the right to use it solely for their own selfish purposes or comfort. Rather, he reminds us that everything comes from God and that without God's constant nurture, nothing would be and nothing could grow. "It is not the gardeners with their planting and watering who count," writes St. Paul, "but God who makes it grow." Indeed, we are not only "fellow-workers" in God's great garden; we ourselves are God's garden (1 Corinthians 3:7-9, REB). This is the ground of our humility as mere creatures among all other creatures loved by God.

Our Christian living ought to reflect an "oikic" ethos. The Greek word *oikos* means a dwelling or a place to live. The words "economy" and "ecology" come from this same Greek word. The *oikumene,* the whole creation, is the church's ethical concern. Our incarnational faith inspires a vision of humankind's relationship to creation that is sacramental, ecological, and ethical. In its elevation of bread and wine, the liturgy of the eucharist makes this connection clear.

The Armenian writer Teotig tells a story about the genocide of the Armenians during World War I. Father Ashod Avedian was a priest of a village near the city of Erzeroum in eastern Turkey. During the deportations, 4,000 Armenian men of that village were separated from their families and driven on a forced march into desolate regions. On their march to death, when food supplies had given out, Father Ashod instructed the men to pray in unison, "Lord have mercy," then led them in taking the "cursed" soil and swallowing it as communion. The ancient Armenian catechism called the *Teaching of St. Gregory* says that "this dry earth is our habitation, and all assistance and nourishment for our lives [comes] from it and grows on it, and food for our growth, like milk from a mother, comes to us from it."

Teotig's story is a reminder that we belong to the earth and that our redemption includes the earth from which we and all the creatures have come, by which we are sustained, and through which God continues to act for our salvation. If water is the blood of creation, then earth is its flesh and air is its breath, and all things are purified by the fiery love of God.

For the earth to bring forth fruit there must be

water and air and the light and heat of the sun. Every gardener knows this, and so recognizes that the right combination of these elements lies beyond the control of science or contrivance. That is the wisdom and agony of gardening. God's creation cannot subsist without God's abundant grace. God has given human beings the sacred responsibility of mediating God's grace and by offering blessings to lift the ancient curse of Adam and expel the demons from every living thing and from the earth and its waters and from the air. No human science or technology can accomplish this, although we are constantly tempted to think so.

So let us be good gardeners and teach our children to be the same. Modern Christians have spoken a lot about "stewardship" of the earth. But I think we are overly practiced at the kind of management that this word easily connotes. We need another perspective, another metaphor. Scripture gives us the symbol of the garden. Adam and Eve were placed in a garden where they walked together with God and did not need to garden. But when they sinned and were expelled, gardening began. Gardening symbolizes our race's primordial acceptance of a responsibility and role in rectifying the harm done to the creation through sin.

The Armenian liturgy speaks of human beings as "co-creators" with God. But what is meant by this expression? Certainly not any kind of equality with God. God alone is the Creator. We are not literally co-creators, but sacramental gardeners. We garden in order to provide sustenance for ourselves and the other creatures. But we also use the fruit of our gardens to prepare the bread of the sacrament. In a petitionary prayer of the Armenian Rite of Washing the Cross, the priest asks: "Bless, Lord, this water with the holy cross, so that it may impart to the fields, where it is sprinkled, harvests, wherefrom we have fine flour as an offering of holiness unto thy Lordship."

The fruit of the garden is not restricted to what we eat. Every garden lends something more to the imagination — beauty. The beauty of a turnip garden may be more homely than the beauty of a tulip garden, but there is beauty in it nevertheless. Every garden holds the potential of giving us a taste of Paradise. Sometimes this comes as a grace that does not exact one's personal labor, but somewhere someone has labored with the sweat of the brow to make the garden grow. There is no ecstasy without first agony.

Jesus prayed in a garden and agonized there, watering it with his tears. His body, which was torn on the Cross, was also buried in a garden. And three days after his crucifixion, the women who wept as he hung on the Cross and anointed our Lord's body returned to that garden to find that the seed which they had lovingly prepared for planting had already borne a sweet and fragrant fruit. Every garden is an intimation of the Garden that is Christ's, that he himself tends in the hearts of those who welcome him in.

> Even today on this earth of thorns
> > we can see in the field
> the spikes of wheat which God,
> > despite those curses, has given:
> cradled with them, the grains receive their birth,
> > thanks to the wind;
> at the will of the most High,
> > who can perform all things,
> does the breeze suckle them,
> > like a mother's breast it nurtures them,
> so that herein may be depicted a type
> > of how spiritual beings are nourished.
> > > St. Ephrem, *Hymns on Paradise*

The sensual breeze that breathes life into our earthly gardens is a type of the spiritual breeze that wafts through the Garden of Paradise. The breeze moves out and into the bitterest and most barren regions in which man and beast dwell. As St. Ephrem says, it "tempers the curse on this earth of ours."

> That Garden is
>   the life-breath
> of this diseased world
>   that has been so long in sickness:
> that breath proclaims that a saving remedy
>   has been sent to heal our mortality.
>
> *Hymns on Paradise*

Last of all, God also has planted within each human being a seed of hope that, if properly nurtured, grows into a confidence that all will be well, all manner of things shall be well. The breath of God reaches into even the smallest and most remote garden and human heart and infuses life. Even more, it brings salvation. The anemone and the rose grow in the earthly garden, but in the Garden of Paradise the anemone grows without the blood of the Cross and the rose has no thorns. The Armenian Epiphany hymn of the blessing of the water declares: "Today the garden appears to mankind,/let us rejoice in righteousness unto eternal life. . . ./Today the shut and barred gate of the garden is opened to mankind."

Let every Christian be a gardener so that he and she and the whole of creation, which groans in expectation of the Spirit's final harvest, may inherit Paradise. If we Christians truly treasure the hope that one day we, like Adam and the penitent thief, will walk alongside the One who caused even the dead wood of the Cross to blossom with flowers, then we must also imitate the Master's art and make the desolate earth grow green.

Lenten Spring

two

Now wind torments the field,
turning the white surface back
on itself, back and back on itself,
like an animal licking a wound.

Nothing but white — the air, the light;
only one brown milkweed pod
bobbing in the gully, smallest
brown boat on the immense tide.

A single green sprouting thing
would restore me. . . .

Then think of the tall delphinium,
swaying, or the bee when it comes
to the tongue of the burgundy lily.

Jane Kenyon, "February: Thinking of Flowers"

WHEN THE EARTH is still damp and cold with melted snow, I kneel at the edge of the perennial bed beseeching the first green blades of the crocuses and daffodils to grow. I drift into my vegetable garden and rake off last year's withered vines. I look down at the dead gray shoots of the asparagus row and try to imagine how in a month's time splendid green spears will break through the mounded earth.

Spring has come slowly this year. But there's work to be done. The vegetable garden needs to be turned and smoothed. The straw blanket that covers the perennial bed should be removed and the remaining old growth cut down. For the gardener the first signs of spring are an irresistible invitation to make the earth a paradise once more.

Gardening and the spiritual life are very much

alike. And as Evelyn Underhill has commented, there are appropriate and inappropriate ways of cultivating both the earth and the spiritual soil of our lives:

> The idea that a good vigorous campaign with a pitch fork is the best way of extirpating tiresome weeds from a herbaceous border is the one we most have to unlearn. We plunge in, toss the ground violently in every direction, pluck out the weeds, make a big pile, and retire in a state of moist satisfaction saying we've done a very good morning's work.
>
> But have we? We've disturbed the roots of the best perennials. We've knocked off some shoots. We've grubbed up loads of little modest seedling. . . . And in our hurry, we've broken weeds and left the bottom half of their stems in the ground to start vigorous life again.
>
> *The Ways of the Spirit,*
> ed. Grace Adolphsen Brame

Every experienced Christian gardener knows that there is a spiritual spring which comes just as surely as nature's spring. The Lenten spring is God's invitation to prayer, fasting, and penance. Like the deep-rooted thistle weed, some of our worst habits withstand all but the most persistent, persevering, and

strenuous exercise. A quick pull on the root, however, will not do the trick, nor will an aggressive
chop of the hoe. Patience is needed, and the humble
willingness to drop down on one's knees and work
carefully with the hand fork and trowel. The Christian gardener patiently picks sin from the soul's soil
and cultivates it with care and attention to the tender new growth of faith.

The Christian gardener also respects the fact that
God appoints each soul to be "the sort of garden it is
to be." "Your job," Underhill admonishes, "is strictly
confined to making [your soul] as good as it can be of
its sort." Some of us will be contemplative in the
manner of a rose garden, and others are more earthy
and restless, like a potato patch. The Christian gardener respects God's prevenient grace in the synergy
of salvation just as she also studies carefully the nature of the plants that grow and gives the appropriate care to each.

The land is poor where I live, and when I first
dug up my vegetable garden, I came to a place where
there wasn't a trace of topsoil, only shale and sand-
stone. It took lots of manure and compost to make
the garden productive, and still each spring I dig up
pails of rocks as if they had grown from stone seeds
all winter long. Then I rake the newly cleared earth
and trace the rows for sowing the seed of spinach,

mustard, and beets. I send each seed into the earth from the tips of my fingers with love, and hope for new life and growth of rich green paradise.

> How Love burns through the Putting in the Seed
> On through the watching for that early birth
> When, just as the soil tarnishes with weed,
> The sturdy seedling with arched body comes
> Shouldering its ways and shedding the
> earth crumbs.
>
> Robert Frost, "Putting in the Seed"

With prayer and fasting in the Lenten spring, the Christian clears the self's soil of stony sin and makes rooms for the birth within of the pierced heart and bleeding flesh of Jesus. "A new heart I will give you, and a new spirit I will put within you; and I will remove from your body the heart of stone and give you a heart of flesh" (Ezekiel 36:26, NRSV). Our love and labor combined with God's grace can make even the poorest stony soil grow round red beets, sweet hearts of flesh.

A Byzantine hymn says, "The Lenten spring shines forth the flower of repentance." The flower of repentance, however, grows only in the soil which has been enriched by the death of the old self that we have let die in it. The Son of God took our sins into the tomb with him, and his body that was planted in a garden bore the fruit of eternal life. When we moved into our home, I made a flower bed in the partial shade of an old wild cherry tree and saved space for my favorite woodland flowers. Early one spring, while hiking, I found a colony of the bloodroot flowers with snow-white blossoms. So I planted some under that tree, and now they bloom each spring. The bloodroot flower rises straight to the sun out of a purple sepulcher of enfolded leaf. At nightfall the elongated finger-figured petals press together prayer-like, searching for the morning light. And after a brief life these perfect petals fall back into the rich brown earth from which they sprang, and in their place rise heart-shaped leaves nourished by a bright orange-red medicinal balm.

The great Maundy Thursday prayer of the Armenian Church says that through "his abundant love" and death on the Cross, Christ gave us "a drug and medicament of repentance." All the Lenten spring I awake to the morning sun and faithfully follow a path of penance that guides me to the bloodroot's bleached blossom and healing ointment. Its white petals remind me of the sinless Lamb of God who bought my salvation, and the tree beneath which that flower blooms also reminds me of another tree or two.

Instead of the budding death-bearing tree that
sprouted in the middle of Eden, you [Christ] carried the wood of the cross up to Golgotha. Receive
my soul, which has fallen in sin and is carrying a
heavy burden, and carry it upon your shoulders
like a lamb, to the promised heavenly place.

"This Ineffable Day,"
A Good Friday hymn
of St. Nersess the Graceful

An important Lenten theme in Orthodox Christian
worship is the expulsion of Adam and Eve from the
garden of delight and our return to it through the
Cross. The Byzantine Vespers service for Tuesday of
the first week of Lent expresses this vision:

Cast out of old from Paradise through eating bitter
food, let us make haste to enter there once more,
abstaining from the passions and crying to our
God: Thou hast stretched out Thy hands upon the
Cross, drunk vinegar and tasted gall, and patiently
Thou hast endured the pain of the nails: uproot all

bitter pleasures from our souls, and in Thy tender mercy save Thy servants.

Once we were cast out of Paradise through eating of the Tree, but through Thy Cross we are restored again to Paradise.

The Armenian Melody hymn for Sundays of Lent also recalls the Garden of Eden: "There in the Garden there were three:/Adam and Eve and the commandment of the Lord." Because they transgressed against the command not to eat of the Tree of the Knowledge of Good and Evil which was in the garden, Adam and Eve forfeited the opportunity God gave them to live a yet more perfect life. Instead, their sin subjected them to that very same death all the other creatures die but which for human beings, who were created by God in his own image and intended by him for immortality, separates them eternally from the presence of God: this is what is meant by the first couple's expulsion from the garden and proximity to the Tree of Life.

In Paradise God exacted no labor from Adam and Eve, except that they tend the garden of their own selves. But they failed in their reponsibility and were subject to nature's entropy, which human beings alone are unable to change.

During the Lenten spring this entropy and process of sinful death are reversed. The Incarnate Word dies a fleshly death and brings new and more abundant life out of that death. During Lent we who call Jesus the Lord of Life retrace his redemptive journey from the refreshing waters of the Jordan River, where he was baptized, to the desert where he denied the devil thrice. In Lenten spring Christians follow Christ's path from the garden of sorrows to the garden of his resurrection. On Good Friday we thirst with Christ on the Cross. We want to drink and refresh ourselves at the living waters that flow from the garden of delight, but to get back to that garden and drink from its living waters we first have to walk through the desert of our own inner spirit.

During Lent and Holy Week the Father beckons us to walk alongside his Son and on that way cast off our sin with prayer and fasting. The rest the Son has done for us. He will meet us at the gates of Paradise. He will carry us through death into new and eternal life. The Tree of Life still stands in the midst of the garden, but the condemnation has been removed. We can approach it and can partake of the life it gives because Jesus, the only pure and holy Sacrifice, was hung on another tree. This is his mercy and his grace.

In the Armenian Church the Melody hymns for Easter are the same as for Ordinary Sundays because in the Christian faith Easter *is* ordinary. And each

week is a journey through ordinary time to the garden and the joy of resurrection.

> The voice of good tidings sang to the women.
> It sounded like the call of the trumpet: —
> "The Crucified whom ye seek is risen! . . ."

> Mary called to the gardener: —
> "Didst thou remove my first born, my love?"
> — "That bird is risen, the wakeful being,"
> Did the Seraph trumpet to the Mother and
>   to those with her,
> — "The savior of the world, Christ is risen!
> And he has delivered mankind from death."

At the foot of my garden path, I have planted hyacinths
of purple and pink and white. Through Eastertide their
blossoms and sweet scent draw me into the garden.

> A bright new flower has appeared this day
>   out of the tomb.
> Souls have blossomed and are adorned
>   with divers hues, and have become
>   green with life.
> The florescence of divine light has bloomed
>   in the spiritual spring.

Armenian Ode
for Easter and Eastertide

Several summers ago my children found two turtles and put them in the vegetable garden. During a thaw the next February, as I was digging up the soggy soil where the peas go, I lifted a heavy mound with my shovel, and then another. The two turtles had burrowed down for winter sleep, and I had rudely awakened them too soon. So I carried them to a corner of the garden where I would not disturb them and dug them in again. When my wife said that she feared the turtles might be dead, I said I did not think so (though I wasn't as sure as I sounded). I insisted that in spring they would come up. And they did in Easter week.

Lilies and hyacinths signify the resurrection, and I can understand why. But I have a pair of turtles that plant themselves in my garden each fall like two gigantic seeds and rise on Easter with earthen crowns upon their humbled heads. With the women at the tomb, I marvel. For "Christ did arise, Christ did awaken/Out of the virgin tomb, out of the tomb of light" (Armenian Ode for Ordinary Sundays). And he leads us back, back into the garden of delight.

Fruits of Pentecost

three

At sound as of the rushing wind, and
sight as of fire,
Lo flesh and blood made spirit
and fiery flame,
Ambassadors in Christ's and the
Father's Name,
To woo back a world's desire.

These men chose death for their life
and shame for their boast,
For fear courage, for doubt
intuition of faith,
Chose love that is strong as death
and stronger than death
In the power of the Holy Ghost.

Christina Rossetti, "Rushing Wind"

I N SPRING Christ brings a new dispensation of
hope out of the winter of our disobedience The divine Word who became flesh renews all of creation.
Christ waters us with the blood that spilled from his
pierced body. Now our lives are "like a watered garden," and we "shall never languish again" (Jeremiah
31:12, NRSV). The garden in which the Lord of Life
was buried grows sweet basil and fragrant lilies.

> My beloved has gone down to his garden,
>   to the beds of spices,
> to pasture his flock in the gardens,
>   and to gather lilies.
> . . . he pastures his flock among the lilies.
>
> Song of Songs 6:2-3, NRSV

I was born in May, and as a child I liked that fact.

It seemed as if everything that had died in winter came to life again in May. I knew my birthday was near from the size of the buds on the embracing branches of the maple tree I climbed. I liked to stretch out among the lilies of the valley that grew wild in our yard, their snow-white bells rang with perfume scent announcing the arrival of spring. This was when my father's gardening began in earnest. Into the raked and leveled soil went the tomato and pepper plants and the eggplants, the squash and cucumber seed, and the beans. The garden plot was being transformed, and I could already steal a taste of its first fruits — round red radishes and crisp green lettuce leaves; I dipped tender new rhubarb shoots in a big bowl of sugar.

Pentecost often comes in May. On Pentecost Orthodox Christians decorate churches and homes with greens and flowers. In the Old Testament, Pentecost was a feast of the first harvest of grain. The Christian Pentecost, however, commemorates the descent of the Holy Spirit upon the apostles who were gathered in the upper room (Acts 2:1-4). The church was planted in the springtime of the year, says St. Ephrem.

> God planted the fair Garden,
>> He built the pure Church . . .
> In the Church he implanted

the Word. . . .
. . . .

The assembly of saints bears resemblance
 to Paradise:
in it each day is plucked the fruit of Him
 who gives life to all.

Hymns on Paradise

On Pentecost, the Spirit rained upon the church. Every living soul upon whom the Spirit rains becomes a fruitful garden like Paradise.

In truth there have been many Pentecosts. The church's Pentecost was foreshadowed at the creation of the world when the "the spirit of God moved upon the face of the waters" and life began (Genesis 1:2). Pentecost also anticipates the last day when everything will be made new by the Holy Spirit. The personal Pentecost of each Christian is his or her baptism and chrismation. This was foreshadowed by the visitation of the Holy Spirit with Mary and the Spirit's descent in the form of a dove upon Jesus in the Jordan River. All of these Pentecosts promise immortal life in Paradise. A hymn to the Holy Spirit in the Armenian rite of baptism proclaims:

The Dove that was sent
came down from high

with great sound and like the flashing of light
he armed the disciples with fire
while they were seated in the upper room.

The Dove [who is] immaterial, unsearchable,
. . . searches the deep counsels of God
and taking the same from the Father
tells of the awful second coming.

Blessing in the highest
to him that proceedeth from the Father,
to the Holy Spirit,
through whom the apostles
drank the immortal cup
and invited the earth to heaven.

Henry Mitchell, in his book *One Man's Garden,*
observes that "it is not important for a garden to be
beautiful" in everyone's eyes. But "it is extremely important for the gardener to think it is a fair substi-
tute for Eden." Perhaps this is an overstatement, or
perhaps it is a theological truth. It is important for
the Christian gardener to see beauty in the garden of
his own self. The model of our perfection is Beauty
and Goodness itself, but the particular aspect of that
beauty might depend upon what sort of garden a·
person is to be. The fire is one, although it has many

tongues of flame. St. Gregory of Nyssa says the "Dove" is the "archetypal Beauty." And the dove is present at Christ's baptism as it is as the Spirit hovering over the Apostles in the upper room on Pentecost. The seventeenth-century poet George Herbert draws these connections gracefully in a poem called simply enough "Whitsunday":

> Listen sweet Dove unto my song,
> > And spread thy golden wings in me;
> > Hatching my tender heart so long,
> Till it get wing, and fly away with thee.

> Where is that fire which once descended
> > On the Apostles? thou didst then
> > Keep open house, richly attended,
> Feasting all comers by twelve chosen men.

> Such glorious gifts thou didst bestow,
> > That th' earth did like a heav'n appear;
> > The stars were coming down to know
> If they might mend their wages, and serve here.

At my baptism I turned my back on the serpent in the first garden, and at my chrismation and every Pentecost thereafter I look upon and listen to the song of that beautiful bird of Paradise whose goodness is a gift to anyone whose eyes see, ears hear, and heart is open to the call.

Adam and Eve were cast out from Paradise, but the memory of Paradise remains. So gardeners try to re-create Paradise in their own yards. The Christian who gardens knows that on Easter the curse and the prohibition imposed upon the first couple have truly been removed. And so at mid-spring Pentecost, as the azalea and irises flame the earth in red, blue, and gold, he is in his imagination transported to a trans-figured territory. "The world is charged with the grandeur of God./It will flame out, like shining from shook foil" (Gerard Manley Hopkins, "God's Gran-deur"). The Christian gardener stands in the midst of Paradise as fiery tongues invite "earth to heaven" and lilacs send up sweet incense with the wind.

At this time in nature's cycle, God grants every gardener the chance to experience the sacrament in the physical garden. The Armenian Melody for Pen-tecost celebrates the earth transfigured in floral col-ors, signifying virtue and immortality.

Give thanks to the Holy Spirit who descended
    this day upon the Apostles.
He armed them by miracle with fire and they
    spake with divers tongues.
By his holy coming the earth blossomed anew,
With fragrant rose and violet and saffron.

He, who cultivated the self's soil with prayer and
penance in the Lenten spring and met the gardener
at the empty tomb on Easter morn, now receives the
Holy Spirit in the hope that virtue and righteousness
might grow in the garden of his own self.

The diligent carry their fruits
    and now run forward
to meet Paradise
    as it exults with every sort of fruit.
They enter the Garden
    with glorious deeds
and it sees
    that the fruits of the just
surpass in their excellence
    the fruits of its own trees.

St. Ephrem
Hymns on Paradise

In his commentary on the Song of Songs, St. Gregory of Nyssa exclaims:

> Do you see . . . the meadow blossoming with flowers? Do you see chastity, shining like a fragrant lily? Do you see the rose of modesty, and the violet, the *good odor of Christ?*. Why not make a garland of these? Now is the time to gather these flowers and adorn ourselves with them.
>
> St. Gregory of Nyssa,
> *Commentary on the Canticle*

At Pentecost the Son sends the Holy Spirit over the earth and into each one of us. Beauty makes us beautiful inside. Each of us is changed into a flower that bears fruit of its own kind within the infinite scope of Beauty. The Armenian *Teaching of St. Gregory* declares that "God, who lacks nothing, arranges his kingdom for his beloved as regions of paradise, a wonderful dwelling near to Him."

When I was a child we lived in a small Cape Cod–style house. At one end of the house, a staircase ascended to the bedrooms with the sloping ceilings and knee-high dormer windows. Beneath one window grew a tall lilac tree. When I misbehaved, my parents sent me to my room. I would scamper up the stairs in tears and be greeted by a sweet fragrance, like burning incense. And so as I lay on my bed I would pray. In child speech I asked God to forgive me and make things better, and I sent my prayers up with the lilac. Today, beneath my bedroom window there is another lilac, and at this time of the year the scent of its purple blossoms greets me with ever sweet surprise and memories of childhood prayers. I have learned that goodness is every bit as much a gift as it is a deed, like the fragrance of lilacs.

During the Lenten spring the hard *struggle* of clearing the self's soil of the weeds of disobedience is what mattered most. In Pentecost season the grace of God rains upon us through no merit of our own. It is God's inexhaustible love. In June I step into the cottage garden where the peonies grow. They surprise me with enormous rose blossoms. Where did they come from? Just a month ago they were under the earth. Oh, I know that I planted them three years ago and that I fed them with bonemeal in March after the last snow. But these flowers are sheer gift. I cannot account for them, nor the joy that they give. My toil in the garden seems unconnected with what I see and smell and feel. It would make more sense to believe — as my grandmother used to insist — that if I pick up the toad in my garden (I saw him yesterday), warts will grow on my hands just as they grow all over him.

In Pentecost season we are given the gift of the Holy Spirit, and that is a great mystery.

> You will be a glorious crown in the Lord's hands,
>   a royal diadem held by your God.
> No more will you be called Forsaken,
>   no more will your land be called Desolate,
> . . . for the Lord will take delight in you,
>   and to him your land will be linked
>   in wedlock.
>
> Isaiah 62:3-4, NEB

St. Paul writes that "the fruit of the Spirit is love, joy, peace, patience, kindness, generosity, faithfulness, gentleness, and self-control" (Galatians 5:22, NEB). These are the spiritual flowers of Pentecost. They blossom in the garden of our lives when we open our hearts to the Spirit of God.

Transfiguration

four

Good captain, maker of the light
Who dost divide the day and night,
The sun is drowned beneath the sea,
Chaos is on us, horribly.
O Christ, give back to faithful souls the light!

Prudentius

. . . Being God, the Divine Spirit refashions
completely those whom
He receives within Himself.
He makes them completely anew.
He renews them in an amazing manner.

. . . .

Being immortal, He gives immortality.
Because He is light that never sets,
He transforms all of them into light in whom He
comes down and dwells.
And because He is life, he bestows life to all.

St. Simeon the New Theologian,
Hymns of Divine Love

I N WINTER I begin planning the garden. God
promised Noah:

> As long as earth lasts,
> seedtime and harvest, cold and heat,
> summer and winter, day and night,
> they will never cease.
>
> Genesis 8:22, REB

But December 1988 was different. In that December
an earthquake rocked the mountains of Armenia, my
ancestral home, and death cast dark shadows over
the land where Noah landed his ark. In an interminable
night of winter and bitter cold, fathers wept
openly for their dead children. My life, too, fell under
a dreadful darkness. Night after night during the
empty purgatorial hours before dawn, my sleep was

interrupted by an agonizing wakefulness. And all the dark day I was seized by an unaccountable anxiety and a terrifying fear that I would lose my children too. My "inscape," in the poet Gerard Manley Hopkins's way of expression, was not a garden any more but a dry and desolate valley swept by a harrowing, hollowing wind blowing incessantly.

An old teacher and friend told me some years hence that while I surely had been in the strangling grip of a depression that winter, the fear of losing my children had not in itself been wholly irrational. There could be nothing more reasonable than for Armenian fathers to fear the loss of their children. In December of 1988, it was an earthquake that buried their children under earth and concrete and twisted metal. But for centuries, culminating in the massacres and genocide of 1915, foreign fathers had murdered Armenian children for nothing more or less than glory and the hatred of a people. I have not forgotten the counsel of that teacher and friend, and it continues to comfort me; but the memories of the fear and the agony of that black winter still awaken me at nights and sneak into the garden with me.

Nonetheless, through the winter of 1989, I waited for spring and brighter days. I counted on God's promise so that I could dig and plant once again in the earth under a warm and welcoming sun. I pushed myself through the annual routine of making up orders from the seed catalogues. But when spring came, I didn't want to go out-of-doors. I looked at the new growth in the perennial bed and did not hope for Paradise. I walked along the borders of the vegetable garden and did not feel like planting. The self which had hoped each spring for renewal in the garden had become a memory mourned. In the winter it had withered and died, like the dried-up stalks of last year.

In late March I finally dragged myself into the vegetable garden and turned over the soil as I had always done and had watched my father do and my grandfather before him. I moved robot-like in slow motion. Every thrust of the spade was a terrible agony. Tying together tall saplings to make tripods for the pole beans was an almost impossible labor. I stood in the midst of the garden gripped by an inexplicable, excruciating inner pain. It was as if I was being crushed from the inside out by a Jupiterian gravity. There were no intimations of heaven in the sensible garden, only hell with the sun my tormentor. I could bear neither heat nor light. I wanted to bury myself with the worm in the loose loamy earth and sleep forever.

Was this what the ancient author of Genesis described when he told the story of the expulsion of Adam and Eve from Eden and proximity to the Tree of Life? Was this the meaning of what the Lord God said to Adam: "Cursed is the ground because of you;/ in toil you shall eat of it all the days of your life;/ thorns and thistles it shall bring forth for you" (Genesis 3:17-18, NRSV)? But I could still pray:

> Creator of Light and fashioner of the night,
> Thou, life in death, and light in darkness,
> hope unto those who wait,
> and forbearance unto those that doubt;
> Thou, who with thy skillful wisdom,
> turnest the shadow of death into morning;
> Thou unending dawn,
> thou sun without setting.
>
> St. Gregory of Narek, *Discourse* 93

Christ Jesus, dispel this darkness from the depths of my soul.

> A man, indeed, who has acquired
>   good health himself,
> and is aware in his mind
>   of what sickness is,
> has gained something beneficial
>   and he knows something profitable;

> but a man who lies
> in sickness,
> and knows in his mind
> what is good health,
> is vexed by his sickness
> and tormented in his mind.
> St. Ephrem, *Hymns on Paradise*

I was that second man in the spring of 1989. I would have to wait months to become the first.

In late April my physician found the right medicine, and in June, when the corn leaped high and stretched its silky sleeves toward the sun, the ineffable light of the Sun had begun to part the clouds that had darkened my mind and disquieted my heart. One day I saw my seven-year-old daughter Victoria in the garden shelling peas, and I realized that something had changed. I could love her again with joy in the light in the garden.

In July cucumber and squash vines lavish green garlands over the garden floor and red ripening tomatoes peek out of their silver cages like rubies on a diadem. In July the barren and wasted valley that was my self began to blossom in exciting colors as passion returned. The season of Transfiguration came, the season of the rose. "The rose like a gem takes its glow, the rose like a gem takes its glow./ From the sublime radiance of the sun, from the sublime radiance of the sun" (Armenian Melody for the Transfiguration). On the mountain the rose shone forth the radiant untransformable light, light without shadow, and dazzled the apostles Peter and James and John. Jesus "was transfigured before them, and his clothes became dazzling white, such as no one on earth could bleach them" (Mark 9:3, NRSV). The Armenian Church's Ode for the Transfiguration announces:

> The divine Light shone this day on
> that mountain.
> Mount Tabor is rejoicing, ah rejoicing,
> ah rejoicing, rejoicing and exulting!
> This day Mount Tabor has flourished
> and is filled with luminous flowers.
> For Jesus blossomed in the body and
> manifested the glory of Adam.

Jesus' Transfiguration on Mount Tabor was not merely an "external" event that the three apostles observed; it was an event that *happened in* them as well (Mark 9:2-8). For a few precious moments, Peter and James and John were also transformed by the light: they were filled with the presence of God and with spiritual eyes saw in Christ the glory of their own transfigured humanity.

Scientists tell us that there is natural light that is invisible to the human eye. The earth's sun radiates light waves whose lengths, long and short, are beyond the range of human vision. And yet, without this invisible light and the warmth it gives, nothing would grow in the physical garden. The saints say that there is also an invisible uncreated light without which the garden that is ourselves cannot live and flourish.

Biblical scholars will question whether the Book of Revelation was authored by St. John the Apostle. But it makes great spiritual sense to believe that he who was with Jesus that day on the mountain in the ineffable light was also the one who recorded this vision in that book:

I saw no temple in the city, for its temple is the Lord God the Almighty and the Lamb. And the city has no need of sun or moon to shine on it, for the glory of God is its light, and its lamp is the Lamb. . . .

Then the angel showed me the river of the water of life, bright as crystal, flowing from the throne of God and of the Lamb through the middle of the street of the city. On either side of the river is the tree of life with its twelve kinds of fruit . . . ; and the leaves of the tree are for . . . healing.

Revelation 21:22-23; 22:1-2, NRSV

In transfigured August, when the sweet peppers turn scarlet and the purple satin skin of the eggplant shimmers in the sensual light, when Jacob's ladder in blue reaches heavenward and the golden sunflower turns to crown the Sun, I was healed. On the mountain "Peter said to Jesus, 'Rabbi, it is good for us to be here'" (Mark 9:5, NRSV). Peter had experienced the transformative power of the untransformable light, light without shadow. And he, speaking for the others, exclaimed that it was good, that this light was life. That's how I felt in my garden under the August Sun. It felt good to be there, not merely good again but good in a way I had not known until that day. "Therein . . . [I] joyfully exalted in gladness without grief, for . . . [I] beheld God always coming down into the garden, through whom . . . [my] soul was impressed by the radiance of the divine light" (Armenian Midday Hymn of the First Sunday of Lent). With St. John, I believed in the new Jerusalem and beheld the Garden transformed within the city's jeweled and glistening walls. I could hope again.

Peter, when he saw Jesus in the company of Moses and Elijah, had wanted to build three tabernacles to contain the light. In my dark spring, without even knowing it, I had fulfilled Peter's wish. In August the naked tripods I had built in the paschal season were transformed into translucent tents of woven green life, suffused with resplendent dappled light — timeless, uncontained, and superabundant. Now I stood amidst them in the garden bathed in the light of the Sun and filled with the Spirit of God. And with Peter I uttered, "Lord, it is good for me to be here!"

Mary in the Garden

five

Hail, from whom alone there springs
the unfading Rose;
Hail, for thou hast borne the
sweetly-smelling Apple.
Hail, Maiden unwedded, nosegay of the only King
and preservation of the world.
Hail, Lady, treasure-house of purity, raising us
from our fall;
Hail, Lily whose sweet scent is known to
all the faithful;
Hail, fragrant incense and precious oil of myrrh.

Byzantine Akathistos Hymn
to the Most Holy Mother of God
from *The Lenten Triodion*

MID-AUGUST in the vegetable garden marks the beginning of the final harvest of tomatoes and corn, peppers, squash, and lima beans. I grow my vegetables in raised beds in tightly spaced rows, so in August the garden floor is covered with a thick quilt of leaves and ripened fruit. Even the fence is draped with emerald garlands and beads of golden squash, and the grapes have begun to ripen purple.

When I was a boy, grapes at the grocery store arrived seasonally. And my mother would wait for the Feast of the Assumption to purchase them. As a child, I imagined that there was a strict rule not to eat grapes before they had been blessed. For in August we kept the Feast of the Assumption of Mary the Mother of God. It commemorates her Dormition (or "falling asleep") and translation into heaven. The Orthodox Church believes that Mary, like her Son, was preserved from corruptible death and bodily decay and lifted immediately to God. On Assumption Sunday my church continues the ancient Jewish practice of blessing the firstfruits of the fall harvest. The rite of the blessing of the grapes promises that "through this blessed fruit we shall receive in our spirit the intelligible grace of [God's] blessing, earning pardon and remission of our mortal sins; to be also worthy of partaking from the Tree of Life. . . . And thus immortalized, we shall in the realm of the immortals forever glorify the Son and the Holy Spirit, now and forever."

The Christian hymns for Assumption Sunday describe Mary as the plant that bears the fruit of immortality. She is the vine, the source of the "inexhaustible joy" enjoyed by "those who were sorrowful because of the tasting of the tree of knowledge." From her "bough" is gathered "the cluster of grapes" (Armenian Midday Hymn for the Assumption) that is pressed into the drink of health and salvation. Gregory of Narek, a tenth-century Armenian saint, speaks of Mary as "the healer of the pangs of Eve." She is "the living Eden," the sacred and healing garden, and her Son is, according to the Byzantine Akathistos Hymn, "the Gardener who cultivates our lives," The Church sings the Song of Songs in praise of Mary's beauty and purity. She is the holy Virgin

whose fertile womb was the first garden that the
Word visited and she is the fountain of life from
which Christ drank:

> You have stolen my heart, my sister . . .
> with just one of your eyes, one jewel
>   of your necklace.
> How beautiful are your breasts, my sister
>   and bride!
>   . . . .
>
> Your cheeks are an orchard of pomegranates,
>   an orchard full of choice fruits:
> spikenard and saffron, aromatic cane
>   and cinnamon
> with every frankincense tree,
>   myrrh and aloes
> with all the most exquisite spices.
> My sister, my bride, is a garden close-locked,
> a garden close-locked, a fountain sealed.
>   Song of Songs 4:9-15, REB

The herb garden hugs the walk that leads out
from our back porch. In two steps I am among the
basil and the bee balm, the rosemary and the thyme,
the hyssop and the sage. The garden breathes sweet
perfumes and pungent scents in my path; the flowers in pastel blue, pink, and white reflect light into

my eyes. The hummingbirds gather Mary's sweet nectar that nourished her infant child. Butterflies light upon the fragrant petal fingers that held him to her breast; Mary the "unfading flower . . . come forth anew from the root of Jesse . . . vessel of the seven-fold gifts of the Spirit; Mother of God and Virgin, we magnify thee" (Armenian Midday Hymn).

God gave us these growing things as signs and symbols of his redeeming love for the whole of creation. "The fruit of righteousness is a tree of life," says the author of the proverb (Proverbs 11:30, REB). The Feast of the Assumption is a harvest of wellness and of fullness of life. Hail Mary, Mother of God! "Hail, for through thee joy shall shine forth:/Hail, for through thee the curse shall cease." Hail Mary, Mother of Light, "earth yielding a rich harvest of compassion; . . . for through thee the fields of Eden flower again" (Byzantine Akathistos Hymn).

I have built a fence around my vegetable garden to keep out the deer and the rabbits. I am the old Adam and a son of Noah whom the beasts of the field fear (Genesis 9:2) and with whom I compete for the fruit of the earth. My garden is not the walled garden of the new Eden that exuberantly holds every living and breathing thing. The fence that keeps the creatures of the field out of my garden is a reminder instead of my exile and alienation from Paradise. All of nature suffers for this: the whole creation is covered with the dark mystery of the knowledge of good and evil and aches with an eager longing for light and life (Romans 8:19-23).

Michael Pollan comments in his book *Second Nature* that "every one of our various metaphors for nature — 'wilderness,' 'ecosystem,' 'Gaia,' 'resource,' 'wasteland' — is already a kind of garden, an indissoluble mixture of our culture and whatever it is that's really out there. 'Garden' may sound like a hopelessly anthropocentric concept, but it's probably one we can't get past." In our day we must restore the images of the garden and the gardener. Every gardener is an imitator of Mary's Son; every gardener is an apprentice of the good Gardener of creation. Gardening teaches us that we belong to nature and are also responsible for it. Human culture and nature's destiny are inextricably intertwined. What we add to nature can contribute to its well-being, as well as our own.

Mary's death and assumption into heaven are eternally joined with her blessed conception and birthgiving, thus completing the revelation of God's great mercy toward all of creation. A Byzantine Vespers hymn for the Feast of the Assumption exclaims:

> O Marvelous wonder! The Fount of life hath been laid in a grave, and the tomb hath become a ladder leading to heaven. Rejoice, O Gethsemane, the holy chamber of the Theotokos. And let us believers shout to her with Gabriel the chief of angels, saying, Hail, O full of grace. The Lord is with thee, granting the world, through thee, the Great Mercy.

The Feast of the Assumption is the "deepest" ecology of all. Mary is the new "ark of God . . . who gave birth to the Element of life, moving from life to life" (Byzantine Vespers for the Falling Asleep of our Lady). Mary with child wordlessly prophesied the Word; willingly she wrapped him in her own blessed body and bore him as a babe into the world. In sorrow she watched him die on a Cross. But the blood that poured from his lacerated flesh made the dead wood blossom and forever waters the earth with the promise of paradise.

The memory of Mary's life, birthgiving, and triumph over death is the vision of a garden in which God walks with us as he did in the beginning — a garden that refreshes with the cleanest water and harbors every kind of living thing. In mid-August the Christian gardener visits Mary in the garden where she rested in sacred slumber. He discovers in her lovely visage the hope that if he gardens well, he may join her Son in Paradise in that consummate crowning season.

The Garden Signed
with the Cross

Oh, sacrament of summer days,
Oh, last communion, in the haze,
Permit a child to join,

Thy sacred emblems to partake,
Thy consecrated bread to break,
Taste the immortal wine!

Emily Dickinson,
"Indian Summer"

Faithful cross, a tree so noble
    Never grew in grove or wood;
Never leaf or blossom flourished
    Fair as on thy branches glowed;
Sweet the wood and sweet the iron
    Bearing up so dear a load.

Ah! relax thy native rigor,
    Bend thy branches, lofty tree!
Melt, O wood, in tender mercy!
    Christ, the King of Glory, see!
Veiled in human sin and sorrow,
    Slain, from sin the world to free.

Fortunatus, "Pange Lingua"

ONE OF MY most vivid childhood memories is of a September when my father made grape wine. All that summer I watched the Concord grapes that grew on the wooden arbor outside of my playroom window ripen in the sun. In September, I helped my father pick big bunches of purple berries and put them in the white enamel tub that my mother had used to bathe my brother and me when we were small. In the cold stone cellar, I stomped grapes with my bare feet. It was different from my mother's baths. This bath bit and stung my flesh.

In the winter the juice soured and my mother was left with lots of red wine vinegar. My father never again tried to make grape wine. Instead, he turned back to bottling the best root beer I've ever tasted.

Forty years have passed. I have been blessed with my own family and learned the sacrifice that love exacts. The memory of my father's failed September experiment has aged like good wine in my heart. And when I partake of it, I am grateful for the gall and the vinegar and the sweet fruit that on the Cross bled the drink of my salvation. George Herbert says in one of his poems:

> Who knows not Love, let him assay
> And taste that juice, which on the cross a pike
> Did set again abroach, then let him say
>   If ever he did taste the like.
> Love is that liquor sweet and most divine.
> Which my God feels as blood, but I, as wine.

It does not matter that the wine turned to vinegar in that winter of my youth. Because of Love, the Cross suffices for our spiritual health and for genuine gladness of heart.

> Blessed are you, Holy Wood, intelligible
>   winepress!
> In you was crushed the heavenly bunch
>   of grapes,
> sufficient for gladdening the heavenly
>   and the earthly.
>   David the Invincible,
>   "An Encomium on the Holy Cross of God"

In the month of September many Christians commemorate the Feast of the Exaltation of the Cross, and in my church Exaltation-tide continues until Advent. The feast originates in the tradition that the true Cross was discovered in Jerusalem, perhaps during excavations for the Church of the Holy Sepulchre in the fourth century. That church was built by Emperor Constantine over the location where from earliest times Christians believed that our Lord was buried. I thought it strange that the church keeps this feast in September. Wouldn't it make more sense for it to be in the spring after Easter? For after the agony of Golgotha and the empty tomb, the Cross, which was a sign of ignominy and death, came to be seen as a symbol of victory and life.

But my garden has revealed hidden meanings. September in the garden comes with a rush like the rogue wave that washes with surprise over the ocean beach. The perennial bed is lit up with pink and purple aster flowers, and mustard chrysanthemums carpet the cottage garden. The vegetable plot is inundated with golden squash, green beans, tomatoes, and scarlet bell peppers. My back aches from bending and picking. The wood has borne its fruit. This is the final harvest; and it is good and plentiful.

But in October the wave retreats. The first frost withers the vines; and the unripened fruit splits open, sending tiny seeds into the cool earth. The wooden stakes that in May I drove into the ground are unclothed once again. Except that now three trees stand in my garden — three crosses that grow out of the earth and rock and are draped with limped forms. When I draw near to the middle cross, it is as if its arms are reaching out to embrace me and lift me into the air. And I notice tender young leaves that have burst from the wood during an Indian summer. One spring I made stakes from fresh saplings and in the fall found green buds and leaves the size of squirrels' ears growing on the wood that I thought was dead and dry.

> Blessed are you, Holy Wood, crowned by Christ,
> that grew on earth, yet spreading your arms rose
> above the arches of the highest heavens,
> and brought forth and carried upon yourself
> the imponderable fruit!
> . . . .

You flowered in the stock of Israel,
and the whole earth was filled with your fruits.
David the Invincible,
"An Encomium on the Holy Cross of God"

Picture in your mind, says St. Bonaventure, "a tree whose roots are watered by an ever-flowing river that becomes a great and living river with four channels to water the garden of the entire Church" (Bonaventure, *The Tree of Life*). This is the Cross, and the Cross is the tree that in the beginning blossomed "in the garden planted by God. It was a comfort to Seth, a presage for the father Adam" (Armenian Melody Hymn for the Feast of the Exaltation of the Cross). And we put our trust in that wood on which our Lord Jesus was nailed. We put our trust in it because it is not dead, because it bears the fruit and drink of eternal life.

Christian poets call the Cross the Tree, and painters have pictured it likewise. St. Bonaventure says it is a "salvation-bearing tree,/Watered by a living fountain," whose "fruit is an object of desire." St. Ephrem the Syrian speculates that the tree in Eden

71

"saw that Adam had stolen" the fruit and "sank into the virgin ground/and was hidden/ — but burst forth and reappeared on Golgotha" *(Hymns on Virginity)*. Thus the fruit which God forbade Adam to eat grows for us to take. What was a forbidden object of desire is now the satisfaction of all of our yearnings for life and love.

September's apple blushes in the cool evening, no longer bespeaking shame or lust but Love in the garden of delight.

> As an apple tree among the trees of the wood,
>> so is my beloved among young men.
> With great delight I sat in his shadow,
>> and his fruit was sweet to my taste.
> He brought me to the banqueting house,
>> and his intention toward me was love.
> Sustain me with raisins,
>> refresh me with apples;
>> for I am faint with love.
>>> Song of Songs 2:3-5, NRSV

The Word himself *was* the first Gardener. In the beginning he planted a tree in the garden of Eden that grew the fruit of immortal life. But the serpent came into the garden and claimed the tree as his own, until the Word took our flesh and reclaimed it. Nailed to that tree he made himself the antidote of sin and death. They who nailed our Lord to the Cross did not know that it was his from the beginning, that the selfsame dead instrument of execution was and is forever more a living tree, the Tree of Life that produces the food and drink of the Kingdom of Heaven.

I am forty-nine years of age, and as I stand in the midst of my garden at this time of the year, it seems to me that my garden and I are at about the same stage in our lives. The squash vines have exceeded the bounds of economy and cling tenuously to the fence. The pole beans are losing their leaves, exposing pregnant pods. The sleeves of corn are curled and cracked like parched tongues.

The garden and I are both over-ripe and, frankly, "going to seed." My middle is spreading and my muscles are shrinking. My hair is dry and turning gray. My children have grown large, like the seed pods on the milkweed, and I can no longer hold on to them. But maybe "going to seed" is not so bad after all — the seed falls into the ground and new plants arise in the spring. What did St. Paul say to the Christians of Corinth who doubted the resurrection? "The seed you sow does not come to life unless it first dies; and what you sow is not the body that shall be, but a bare grain of wheat perhaps, or something else; and God gives it the body of his choice; each seed its own particular body" (1 Corinthians 15:36-38, REB).

In the spring a seed was planted, and it bore the firstfruits of the final harvest. "As in Adam all die; so in Christ all will be brought to life; but each in proper order; Christ the firstfruits, and afterwards, at his coming, those who belong to Christ" (1 Corinthians 15:22-23). So at the end of the gardening season, when the leaves of the sugar maple turn canary yellow and flutter in flocks onto the browning earth, Christians remember the Cross. In November, as Advent draws near, look up! — hundreds of wooden crosses reach to the horizon and the birds find rest in them.

When the year grows old, we remember the Cross, only now with the assurance that soon the babe will be born, that the spring is not far off, and that at the last trumpet, at the beginning of Eternal Spring, the Son will clothe our dry bones with new flesh, like the silvery green leaves that burst from the buds on the branches of the maple trees in May.

One cool September morning as I worked in my

garden and the sun was rising, a flock of Canadian geese flew high above. Dozens of small crosses, like the ones pilgrims carve by candlelight on the walls of holy shrines. Only they were spread in a vast V across a luminous sky.

In the Juvenescence
of the Year

The seed is in the ground.
Now may we rest in hope
While darkness does its work.

Wendell Berry,
from *A Timbered Choir*

My life is like a faded leaf,
    My harvest dwindled to a husk:
Truly my life is void and brief
    And tedious in the barren dusk;
My life is like a frozen thing,
    No bud nor greenness can I see;
Yet rise it shall — the sap of Spring;
    O Jesus, rise in me.

Christina Rossetti,
"A Better Resurrection"

AT ADVENT-TIME icy snowflakes play timpani on the last leathery leaves that cling to the branches of the young pin oak in the backyard. The year is old and the earth has grown cold. My garden has turned brown to gray. The cornstalks have shrunk and are crouched over like a platoon of crooked old men. The squash vines have shriveled; their rotted fruit drop seeds to the ground. My turtles have covered themselves with a six-inch earthen comforter. Only the curly kale stands up straight and green, waiting for winter's first white blanket of protection from a harsher freeze.

On a chilly overcast Saturday, I wrestle into my mud-caked boots and trudge out to the vegetable garden. I push open the gate and survey a scene of desolateness. Summer's sensuous celebrants are skeletons and dry bones. I pull up the tomato stakes and

the dead vines. I cut down the cornstalks and pile
them in a corner of the garden. They'll make mulch
for next year's crop, and in the span of a season give
back to the earth what they took.

Where have all the flowers gone? The perennial
beds have lost their raiment, no more wild summer
gaiety of bright colors, the dancers are all undressed
and their feet are frozen in the ground. I cut back the
leggy asters and phlox and dig out the apron of grass
that has encroached on the border's edge. This year
I'll bury a hundred tulip bulbs in a new bed I've dug
just off the back corner of the garage where the lilacs
grow. Into the dark cold November earth they go,
until the sun returns and resurrects them in April.

What did our Lord say? "Except a corn of wheat
fall into the ground and die, it abideth alone: but if it
die, it bringeth forth much fruit" (John 12:24, KJV).
Caryll Houselander has written in *The Reed of God*
that "Advent is the season of the seed." Homely seeds
are pregnant with the mystery of faith and the
promise of radiant new life. The Lord of Creation has
become a small seed inside the Woman's womb. As
"the virgin earth gave birth to . . . Adam, head of the
earth," so "the Virgin [gives] birth to [the new and
second] Adam, head of heaven" (St. Ephrem, *Hymns
on the Nativity*). The Messiah springs up "like a young
plant whose roots are in parched ground" (Isaiah

53:2, REB). He will seed the earth with his wounded love, and his harvest will be a hundredfold (Mark 4:20).

We have spoiled Christmas — maybe lost it — because we have forgotten the meaning of Advent: of the light that comes into the darkness, of our need to repent and prepare ourselves to receive the true gift. Advent is a time to let our old used-up sinful selves die into the earth like the crumpled cornstalks in my garden. Let the reaper come and cut me down, and I will fall to the ground.

In our race to capture just a piece of manufactured happiness we have forgotten that in this captive world the other side of real joy is sorrow. There is dying in the birth of Christ, as there is also birth in his death. Advent and Christmas are about just this. If only we were more attentive. T. S. Eliot captures the meaning in "Journey of the Magi":

> Birth or Death? There was a Birth, certainly,
> We had evidence and no doubt. I had seen
> birth and death,

But had thought they were different;
    this Birth was
Hard and bitter agony for us, like Death,
    our death.

Eastern icons of the nativity picture the grotto in which the child lies as a triangle of absolute darkness, signifying the night of sin into which the Sun brings his light. The innocent child is the crucified Messiah who "descended on earth in order to save Adam, . . . and not finding him there, [went] into hell to look for him" (Byzantine Canticle for Holy Saturday, from *The Lenten Triodion*). The babe's swaddling clothes are also the winding cloths that he leaves behind in the empty tomb and that the angel points out to the spice-bearing women on the third day.

The innocent child born in the darkness of winter and the dying man hung on the leafless tree are the same person: his baptism and resurrection are folded into one another as the petals of the rose. Winter is the season of "the death of air . . . the death of earth . . . the death of water and fire." But on Christmas, the "drawing of this Love and the voice of this Calling" invite us to return "through the unknown, remembered gate" where "the last of earth left to discover/Is that which was the beginning" (T. S. Eliot, "Little Gidding"). In the wintertime of the year, when we least expect, someone invites us to enter verdant Paradise. There the rivers flow peacefully and nourish the earth constantly, swallows sail on a gentle breeze that always refreshes, and the earth yields abundant life in the light of the Sun who never sets. He is the Gardener who wears a laurel wreath jeweled with the sweetest fruit and scented flowers; his wreath encircles the whole earth.

We have tamed Christmas, and domesticated it. We have taken all of the terror and cold out of that night with our electrified lights; and real joy escapes us. We compensate, we cover our silent despair with gay Christmas wrapping. But we know all too well that at the appointed hour the wrappings will all be torn away and crumpled in piles, and our lives will be no different after the day is done. We want the joy of our life without the pain of his birth, or the agony of his crucifixion, or the judgment when he returns. But I ask you: "Why in this season does the holly bear its red berries?"

> Blessed is he
>> for whom Paradise yearns.
> Yes, Paradise yearns for the man whose goodness
>> makes him beautiful.
>
>> St. Ephrem, *Hymns on Paradise*

It is a wonderful thing to know that Paradise yearns for *us*. The words "whose goodness makes him beautiful" are also comforting. Paradise waits for us to grow into plants that bear beautiful flowers and fruits of compassion and love. We are the Christmas tree, and the ornaments with which we adorn it are the virtuous fruits of our own living.

Adam was not made for Paradise, but Paradise was made for Adam. What goodness there must have been in Adam's breast when he was created, and what even greater beauty was restored in us by the perfect Image of the Father who took our nature. "Truth in mankind," St. Ephrem continues,

> surpasses [Paradise's] plants,
> and love is more comely . . .
>> than [Paradise's] sweet scents.
>
>> *Hymns on Paradise*

In the winter that robs the branches of fruit,
the Fruit sprang forth for us from the

barren vine.
In the frost that stripped all the trees
a Shoot budded for us from the house of Jesse.
In January when seed hides in the earth,
the Staff of life sprang up from the womb.

St. Ephrem,
Hymns on the Nativity

I visit my garden in December lest I forget the dying in Christ's birth and the birth in his dying. That is why the early church placed the celebrations of Christ's birth and baptism together in the same season. The Armenian Church even continues to celebrate both the nativity and the baptism of our Lord on the very same day, January 6 (Eastern Epiphany). An ancient Armenian hymn makes the connection:

Light of light, from the Father wast thou
    sent
and wast made flesh of the holy Virgin,
that thou mightest renew afresh the lost Adam.
. . . .

Renewing the old man doth the Savior
    to-day
come unto baptism in order to make new
by water our corrupted natures,

bestowing on us instead the incorruptible
 raiment.
 Christ is baptized, and all creatures are
  hallowed.
Grant then to us remission of sins,
hallowing us anew with water and spirit.

 We tremble at this Light that chases out
  the darkness and the cold.
 We fall down before this Sun which consumes
  the thistle and revives the rose.

        stanza in italic mine. V.G.

In Maryland during early February the daffodils' first pale green spears thrust through the
hardened earth. "A new flower buds forth from the
root of Jesse." For the Mother of Earth, the Queen
of Heaven, "hast given birth to the joy of the
world" (Armenian Melody for the Feast of the Nativity). Forty days after he was born (in accor-
dance with Jewish religious practice), Mary and
Joseph brought Jesus to be blessed at the Temple
in Jerusalem (Luke 2:22-40). At the beginning of
February, many Christians mark this moment in
our Savior's life. The Feast of the Presentation of
the Lord is the final celebration of Christmas, and
it reminds us one last time that the joy of Christ-

mas is bought at a hard price. By his death on the barren tree the Life and Joy of our lives gave us the gift of eternal life. "Simeon blessed them and said to Mary, 'This child is destined to be a sign that will be rejected; and you too will be pierced to the heart'" (Luke 2:34-35, REB).

Christmas is about God's gift of unselfish love, Christ's gift of himself to us. All of our gifts are a way of saying, "Thank you." All of our gifts ought to be in Christ's spirit of unselfish love. The hardest thing to give away is what I love the most, to share completely with others what gives me the greatest pleasure. In the garden our Lord begged the Father, "My Father, if it is possible, let this cup pass by me" (Matthew 26:39, REB). I do not think that it was fear of suffering or even death that moved our Lord to issue this plea to the Father; rather, the love of living his life as one of us moved him to utter this prayer.

When I was a young boy growing up in Connecticut, on warm spring days and cool summer evenings, when a refreshing breeze blew off Long Island Sound, I would take my wiffle bat and ball out

87

to our big side yard. And I would make believe that a game was being played — the New York Yankees, my team, against the Boston Red Sox. Mostly, the Yankees would win. But there was a danger, because at the border of the yard was my mother's flower garden, and right on the other side of a hedgerow was the Wilsons' yard. Mr. Wilson prized his vegetable garden very much. Sometimes, I would be struck with terror, not so much when the ball landed among my mother's flowers, because she was my mother and she would forgive me, but when it bounced into Mr. Wilson's vegetable garden. Then I would scout to see whether he was out, and if the way was clear, slip trembling through a hole I had made in the hedge, just right for a small dog or little boy, and I would scamper about on all fours in Mr. Wilson's garden searching for my wiffle ball. Sometimes, however, Mr. Wilson caught me!

Every gardener knows the temptation. He loves his garden too much. He wants it perfect and unblemished and all for himself. There is this absolute desire for the impossible perfection of the mind's eye and rage at the intruder who spoils it. Had it not been a little boy who disturbed Mr. Wilson's seed rows or crushed the young bean plants, it might have been the rain or the hail, a deer or some rabbits.

And Mr. Wilson would have been just as enraged at these unwelcome "intruders" as with me. He wanted the garden perfect and for *himself*.

What am I doing speaking of spring and summer? They seem a long way off from winter and Christmas. But maybe not so far off. Let me finish with one last story, or at least the main lines of it. It was written by Oscar Wilde for every gardener, and maybe, especially, for every Christian gardener.

Once upon a time there was garden much like yours or mine, only perhaps even more lovely, and it belonged to a Giant. For seven years the Giant was gone to visit an ogre friend in another part of the country. And during that time, the children in the neighborhood had made the garden their special playground. But when the Giant returned and saw the children in his garden, he was very angry. "What are you doing there," he cried. He was a very selfish giant. "My own garden is my own," he yelled out to them. "Anyone can understand that I will allow nobody to play in it but myself." And so he built a very high wall around his garden so that no one could get in.

The next spring, however, something strange occurred. Spring visited every garden in the country except the Giant's garden. He could not understand why his peach trees were not in bloom — there were twelve in his garden — nor any of the other flowers. Then one morning the Giant was awakened by the exquisite song of a bird, and when he looked out his bedroom window the Giant saw that the children had crept into his yard through a small hole in the wall and were playing in the trees in the garden. And wherever the children were climbing the limbs of the trees were covered with blossoms and flowers poked their heads through the green grass below. The Giant's heart melted, and he realized how selfish and unhappy he had been.

But when the children saw the Giant they all ran away, all except a little boy standing by a tree which was not in bloom and whose eyes were so filled with tears that he did not see the Giant coming. Then the Giant took the boy gently in his hand, and put him in the tree. In the wink of an eye the tree was filled with beautiful blossoms and the birds flew to it and broke into song, and the little boy hugged the Giant around his neck and kissed him.

Then the Giant took an ax and knocked down the wall. And from that day on and for many years the children came there to play. The Giant, however, never again saw that special little boy. Yet of all the lovely children that visited his garden the Giant loved him and longed to see him the most.

Many years went by, and the Giant grew old. Then one winter morning the Giant saw something wonderful, and he could hardly believe what his eyes were seeing. In a far corner of the garden one tree was covered with the loveliest white blossoms, and under that tree stood the little boy he had loved so much. With great joy in his heart, the Giant went out to greet the boy. But when he drew near to the child, the Giant saw that in the palms of the child's hands were the prints of two nails, and on his feet the same thing. And the Giant's face grew red with rage, and he said, "Who dared to wound thee? I will take my sword to him and slay him." "Nay," said the child, "but these are the wounds of Love." And the Giant said, "Who art thou?" and he knelt before the child. Then the child smiled on the Giant, and said to him, "You let me play once in your garden, today you shall come with me to my garden, which is Paradise."

I left out one small detail from Oscar Wilde's story of *The Selfish Giant*. Wilde writes that the Giant in his old age "did not hate the Winter now, for he knew that it was merely the Spring asleep, and that the flowers were resting." In the juvenescence of the year the babe in the manger is asleep and resting, but soon he will awaken and with his wounded love will warm the frozen earth. Already in my garden the crocuses are ready to bloom.

Acknowledgments

The author gratefully acknowledges the following sources:

Agat'angeghos, *The Teaching of Saint Gregory: An Early Armenian Catechism,* translated by Robert W. Thomson, Harvard University Press, © 1970.

Wendell Berry, Poem V, 1991 (p. 78), from *A Timbered Choir,* copyright © 1998 by Wendell Berry. Reprinted by permission of Counterpoint Press, a member of Perseus Books LLC.

Bless, O Lord: Services of Blessing in the Armenian Church, Diocese of the Armenian Church of America, © 1989.

Bonaventure, translated by Ewert Cousins, Classics of Western Spirituality Series, Paulist Press, © 1978.

Emily Dickinson, "Indian Summer," *Collected Poems of Emily Dickinson,* Avenel Books, 1982.

The Divine Liturgy of the Armenian Apostolic Orthodox Church, translated by Tiran Archbishop Nersoyan, Saint Sarkis Church, London, © 1984.

T. S. Eliot, excerpt from "Little Gidding" in *Four Quartets,* copyright 1942 by T. S. Eliot and renewed 1970 by Esme Valerie Eliot; reprinted by permission of Harcourt Brace & Company and Faber & Faber Ltd.

T. S. Eliot, excerpt from "Journey of the Magi" in *Collected Poems, 1909-1962* by T.S. Eliot, copyright 1936 by Harcourt Brace & Company, copyright © 1964, 1963 by T. S. Eliot; reprinted by permission of Harcourt Brace & Company and Faber & Faber Ltd.

"An Encomium on the Cross" from *David Anhagt': The "Invincible" Philosopher,* edited by Avedis Sanjian, Scholars Press, © 1986. Reprinted by permission of The University of California.

Saint Ephrem, *Hymns on Paradise,* translated by Sebastian P. Brock, St. Vladimir's Seminary Press, © 1990. Reprinted by permission of St. Vladimir's Seminary Press.

Ephrem the Syrian: Hymns, Introduction by Kathleen E. McVey, Classics of Western Spirituality Series, Paulist Press, © 1989.

Saint Gregory of Nyssa, "Commentary on the Canticle," *From Glory to Glory: Texts from Gregory of Nyssa's Mystical Writings,* St. Vladimir's Seminary Press, © 1979. Reprinted by permission of St. Vladimir's Seminary Press.

George Herbert, "The Agony," *The Complete English Works,* Everyman's Library, Alfred A. Knopf, 1995.

Jane Kenyon, "February: Thinking of Flowers," © 1996 by the Estate of Jane Kenyon. Reprinted from *Otherwise: New and Selected Poems* with the permission of Graywolf Press, St. Paul, Minnesota.

The Lenten Triodion, translated by Mother Mary and Kallistos Ware, Faber & Faber Ltd, © 1984.

Prudentius and Fortunatus were quoted from the *Macmillan Book of Earliest Christian Prayers,* edited by F. Forrester Church and Terrence J. Mulry, Macmillan, © 1988.

Saint Simeon the new theologian, *Hymns of Divine Love,* translated by George A. Malloney, reissued by Dimension Books, PO Box 811, Denville, NJ 07834, © 1975.

Evelyn Underhill, *The Ways of the Spirit,* edited by Grace Adolphsen Brame, Crossroad Publishing Co. Inc., © 1993.

Oscar Wilde, "The Selfish Giant," *Oxford Book of Modern Fairy Tales,* edited by Alison Lurie, Oxford University Press, © 1993.